I0510570

"BE LIKE APPACHE

or a short guideline on the coaching process".

Artur Tolloczko

Preface

W hat an intriguing title I thought when I saw this book for the first time. Appache Winnetou

is my childhood hero who personified all the positive qualities I could have, at the time,

imagined. Everyone wanted to be like him, to traverse on the horse's back through prairies, feel freedom, fight for a just cause, defend the weaker and measure out justice. In short, the pattern of virtues, all sorts. Anyway, up till now the values that he personified are extremely important to me.

All good... just what does my childhood hero have to do with coaching?

I'm a coach, I should know it. I have been involved in this field for more than 15 years. Although it seems a lot, somehow nothing came into my head. It encourages me even more to start reading. The mystery has already been explained in the first part of the book, but it has not at all impeded my curiosity. Because the story which you will start to read in an extremely simple and clear way, with no superfluous words (and let's remember that Winnetou himself he was rather taciturn and restrained) explains the essence of coaching.

The form is also interesting because it is a synthetic record of a coaching session that never took place, but in my experience, that a very similar session could happen more than once.

Winnetou once said that the future is like a book that has not yet been read.

Coaching is mainly about an unknown future.

Participating in coaching sessions, the client creates his own future, that is, instead of waiting for a predetermined one, created already in someone's book, he writes it for himself. In the way, as much as possible, to fulfil his own expectations.

There is also a large group of people, of course, who for some reason choose, maybe not fully consciously, existing books, thinking that there is no other option. They then live a history already created for them by someone else. Sometimes these others are parents, sometimes a husband or a possessive boss. But Beata, or the heroine of this story, chose a different path, she decided to create her own path in life, word after word, chapter after chapter. And how she created her own story you'll find out in a moment.

Rafał, Coach of ICC coaching

C oaching is very popular and this is no surprise as it is simply effective.

It helps to discover and define what your heart's desire may be. It ensures you make the right decisions. It shows how and where to look for energy to attain commitments.

If any business, education or educational process you experience in life, will be strengthened by coaching, then we can expect good effects much faster.

The method alone does not guarantee a result, it is

rather the coach's knowledge and experience combined with openness and customers' determination which is the key to success.

You can read a lot about coaching. There are plenty of specialist reports, interesting research and scientific positions on this subject. The advantage of a book that you hold in your hands is the reality that flows from the coaching practice of the author. Easy to read and straight to the point. Although the main character is a fictional person, I can say with certainty, that each of the described chapters took place during my coaching sessions.

My favourite metaphor of coaching is short: to put you on the right path. I have been dealing with this since 2007 and define coaching as a professional supportive relationship.

There are three key aspects.

First of all, to support and strengthen the person who is seeking coaching so it makes him conscious, strong and independent.

Secondly is the relationship. Coaching is the art of establishing a dialogue between

the coach and client. The interaction that takes place between them serves the client in achieving his goals. I illustrate this dependence by some old wisdom which says that just as iron is sharpened with iron, one man shapes another.

And so we come to the third aspect. Supporting a

relationship must be professional, because coaching is also a profession, which is becoming more and more popular. Not everyone is a professional coach, not everyone has graduated from coaching school and has certifications and diplomas, but each supporting coaching relationship should be led by specified principles of cooperation, clear division of roles and responsibilities, a specific course and its beginning and end.

Artur described the method in a simple and transparent way how to support others with coaching. Reading his book you can easily get to know the key elements of a coaching conversation and tools, which a coach uses during the process. You will find it all in the book you keep in your hands.

In a book that 'will put you on the right path', on the go into the world of coaching.

Dawid, PCC ICF, Executive Coach & Coach Trainer

Admission.

F irst of all, thank you and congratulations that you reached this position. This means that you are in a prestigious group of people who are interested in the subject of coaching, or maybe are in the coaching process or even intend to become coaches and in this way help others.

A lot of people I met on my coaching path, associates coaching with reprimand and control, not support and help. For this reason, I decided to write this short textbook. I hope, that it will help change the perception of this great development tool.

The purpose of this book is to show the main rules concerning the course of coaching sessions, the answer to the question of how coaching works, what it is, what the types of coaching are and how it can help me.

To present the topic in an interesting form, I have decided to write this short textbook in the form of reports from fictional sessions with a fictitious person, that can be a classic representation of someone who needs help that coaching is able to give.

In no way is this a full description of what happens during coaching. There is no place for it, nor possibilities. Each session is very individual and something unique. In addition to words, emotions arise.

Body language, intonation, reveal much more than words alone can express. A coaches uses techniques, relevant questions, but is also guided by intuition, the need of the moment. Depending on the process stage other tools may be incorporated. That's why I encourage you to read the following chapters with the hope that after reading you will find answers to the questions; what is coaching? How it goes and most importantly: how can it be helpful for me? I encourage you to read it.

Artur Tolloczko. Warsaw 2019.

"BE LIKE APPACHE

or a short guideline on the coaching process".

"WHY DO I NEED COACHING?"

The first chapter in which we find out what the coach does and why Beata needs his help.

"**W**hat is the reason you have decided on coaching?" After a few minutes of polite exchange of opinions, the coach has passed to the point.

Beata fell into thoughts. The question is simple, but the answer not so much anymore. What should she say? Is it about how she learned about coaching and what convinced her to accept this particular offer? Or maybe it is about all the doubts she is struggling with from time to time. It occurred to her that maybe it's best to get started right away with the task of this most important question, with which she came.

"You know," she began, "I recently received an email with your offer. Do you remember what was there? If you want to take important life decisions, if you just got promoted. If in your life there has been a change that you cannot deal with. If you are standing at a crossroads and you do not know which direction to take ..." she smiled. "I do not remember the exact content, but I think that it sounded more or less like that. I know that after reading it I realised that these words were aimed at me. I am just at the moment when I have to take an important life decision."

"Do you have to, do you want to?" the coach interrupted.

"I think... that I want," she decided after a short reflection. "Yes, I definitely want to."

She smiled again.

"Tell me please what is the reason why people are usually applying for coaching? What is it all about this coaching? Maybe it's stupid that I'm asking about it now that I've come to you. But about coaching I know only this, that it is some kind of support and that there are several varieties of it."

The coach smiled at Beata's honesty.

"It's true that there are several kinds of coaching. I deal with life and business coaching and also executive coaching for managerial staff. All three are defined as types of holistic coaching, that is, dealing with human needs. I can also go to the field and do operational coaching. I prefer to deal, not only with business issues, but with the whole person and I mean it in very wide terms. Even when we focus on specific business needs, e.g. 'how to improve communication with my partner', we still touch the area of human needs."

Beata nodded.

"I understand that many issues are closely related to each other."

"Exactly." The coach painted a circle in the air. "A man with his way of thinking, individual habits, attitudes, image of the world, feelings and needs. It is a whole. These individual elements act as a system of connected vessels. Some areas affect others. That's why we're talking about holistic coaching."

"And this operational kind?"

"Operational or tool coaching relies on staying with a client in his natural environment of work. It is based on observation of his actions and later on a conversation that aims to improve efficiency of these activities. The whole secret of effective coaching in the field lies in focusing on positives. Looking for positive elements in the client's work and then focusing on improving efficiency based on these positive features. We often exercise and observe techniques and tools used at work, hence the name 'tool'." The coach gesturing has become dynamic. It was obvious that he liked the subject.

"Let's look at an example. If a seller was great at building a relationship with one client but does not go well with another, then we can analyse these elements. What enabled him to achieve success in the first case and think about what hindered achieving the same effect in the second. In this kind of coaching process it is even allowed to advise, whether a demonstration of how you can do things better is needed. So you can enter into mentoring elements, consulting and training. We do not usually do this in holistic coaching."

"How is it? You do not advise anything to the client during coaching?" Beata asked with undisguised amazement. "So how are you able to help him?"

"Holistic coaching assumes that nobody knows better a given situation than the client himself who is involved in it. Nobody knows better than him about delicate nuances in the area of relations or political relationships there. Therefore, the best answer to the main coaching question is residing inside the client. What belongs to the tasks of the coach, it is skilful to bring it out in the open."

"It makes sense. Who knows my situation better, than me alone?" Beata smiled showing nice white teeth.

"And what about my other question: for what reason people most often ask for coaching?'"

"You have already mentioned the main reasons, quoting my mailing. The manager is promoted and encounters many new matters to him. He needs to sort them out, find answers to the questions: 'how to deal with this or with that'. Someone else might have a great idea, but he does not know how to get to realisation. Someone else has a dream and he needs someone who will analyse with him, the process of reaching the assumed goal. Occasionally someone comes along who suddenly finds himself in an unusual, difficult situation to him and needs someone who will look at it from the outside and without emotion" The coach shrugged his shoulders. "As you can see, there are many reasons. The most important thing is to know what your reason is, what is the real question you want to find the answer to. If you know it, the coach should help you to find an answer. The more important the question, the more valuable it becomes. However, if in your personal life and at work everything is sorted, it means that at this time you do not need such support."

"I understand. So that you could help me, there must exist a topic which I want to face."

The coach smiled broadly.

Will Beata feel sympathetic to the coach and decide to take further sessions? About this and about the first principle of successful coaching in the next

Artur Tolloczko

chapter.

"DO I WANT TO SPEAK WITH HIM?"

The second chapter in which we find out how important the first impression is and how much you depend on it in coaching.

The waiter has brought ordered coffee.

"The first thing we have to determine now is whether you accept me as your coach." The coach began.

Beata looked up.

"What do you mean? Is it not enough that I am already here and talking to you?"

"The coaching process usually consists of approximately six to seven sessions in two or three week intervals. Each session is approximately one to one and a half hour. And there is homework ,e-mails and telephone contacts. All this means that we will be in quite intense contact for three or four months."

The coach sipped his coffee wetting his lips.

"For this reason your feelings are extremely important from the first meeting. You know that seeing someone for the first time you already feel sympathy or dislike for him. The first impression very much affects the quality of further relationship. Of course, it works in both ways" he added.

Beata looked up.

"Both ways?"

"Yes." The coach confirmed with a nod. "Sometimes it happens that I refuse a client if I see that it is difficult for us to communicate at the first meeting."

"There are other reasons why you refuse?"

The coach smiled broadly.

"Two more: when the customer does not pay, and when I think that he needs the help of a psychotherapist not mine, which happens from time to time."

"What's your decision for me? Would you like to continue working with me?" Beata looked on slightly uptight.

"Of course I do. – The coach nodded with a smile -

Be like Appache or a short guideline on the coaching pro-

more importantly; do you?"

"Of course, let's get started. I'm already curious what will happen next."

They both sat down more comfortably.

Will Beata accept the rules of co-operation with the coach?

About this in the third chapter.

"CONTRACT"

The third chapter in which we will find out what differentiates a coach from a priest and we will get to know four principles of co-operation between the coach and the client.

"**A**t the beginning, we should set out the rules. So called 'contract'."

"Aha. So how much I have to pay you, yes?" Beata thought it was strange to start with money, but on the other hand, she wanted to put it behind her.

"That too," The coach said with a smile. "But it is also important to set the rules on which we will be working. First of all," he started counting on his fingers, "I assume you have all the resources you need, to achieve the assumed goal of the session and I want you to know that the responsibility for achieving this goal rests on you. Do you understand what I mean?"

"You are telling me that if I do not try hard during the sessions and will not put the right effort to achieve the goals that we set for ourselves, we will not be able to achieve them?"

She answered with slight hesitation.

"I say we can manage it if you try hard and put in effort to achieve them" corrected the coach.

Beata laughed loudly.

"Almost the same, but this 'almost' makes a difference" she admitted.

The coach nodded seriously.

"It is true. The way we approach goals is extremely important. If we formulate them positively, we will give a signal of our sub consciousness, that we really want to implement them."

"It's a bit complicated, but I accept. What's next?" Beata's interest grew.

"Because the responsibility for achieving the goal on your side, I am responsible for the proper course of the process."

"That sounds fair," she said, nodding.

"Thirdly" the coach continued. "Everything about

what we will speak here, stays between us."

"As with a priest?"

"Exactly."

"I like it. What else?"

"Fourth, you have the right not to answer my questions and not to do the tasks I ask you. You can also tell us to finish the drilling of the theme. Do you accept these rules?"

"Yes, I accept," Beata said, this time very seriously.

"Great. We'll talk today about the main goal you want to achieve. If you decide

to continue our co-operation, (for today's time you do not pay anything), we'll sign the contract in which we will determine the number and price of the sessions. Agreed?

"Of course" Beata was pleasantly surprised that the first meeting was free.

How will Beata start talking about her goal?

Will the coach help her determine what she wants to achieve meeting him? About that in the next, fourth chapter.

"WHAT WILL WE BE SPEAKING ABOUT?"

The fourth chapter in which blows hot wind from the prairie and we will start to discover Beata's goals.

The coach pulled out a thick green notebook.

"If you do not mind, I will make some notes during our meetings. If you want, after the sessions we will destroy them together" he looked at Beata.

"Of course. I do not mind" Beata imagined the green notebook getting burned in the fireplace.

"Okay. It's time for the most important question

that will show us what we will be doing on our next meetings. What is your goal? What do you want to achieve by this process?"

Beata slightly lowered her eyes. Actually, she did not know how to answer this question, so she started from the beginning.

"Do you know what I was dreaming about when I was a child?"

She asked quietly.

The coach shook his head.

"I wanted to be an Indian. I dreamed of living in a wigwam in the Wild West, ride on a white horse on a prairie and feel hot wind in my unkempt hair. I wanted to be Winnetou." She blushed slightly, but she continued.

"You know, I was a scout. I went to camps. I went sailing on yachts. I slept in a tent by lakes and in the mountains. That was during primary, secondary school, university ... and then it started 'work'."

She was silent for a moment. The coach did not interrupt the silence.

"I worked hard. It paid off. I was promoted. In practice, I was promoted every two years. Today I am the director of a large department. I've become Winnetou ..." she smiled, but her eyes betrayed sadness.

"I guess that what you have achieved in the end has

not been fulfilment of your dreams?"

"You're so right," she said quietly. "I manage. I am a boss, a leader. But I miss something there", she pointed out at heart. "More and more often I think about the prairie, about the unkempt hair, about real Winnetou."

"What would you like to achieve during our meetings?" The coach asked after a moment of silence.

Beata looked him straight in the eye.

"I cannot give up my job. I have a daughter, who I look after by myself. However, I would like to feel the wind while sailing again, somehow I want to fill this empty space in my heart."

"Please, confirm whether I understand you well. You want to find a way to be able to continue to fulfil your director's duties but also fill the need in your heart and feel like Winnetou from your dreams. Correct?"

"Exactly. You put it right."

"Do you know the SMART acronym?"

"Of course" Beata shrugged.

"I am asking you now to put this goal in the SMART framework, so that it would be specific, measurable, ambitious but realistic and preferably also defined in time."

"It's difficult, but I will try." Beata raised her cup of coffee to her lips. While she was drinking, for a moment she looked like her thoughts were wandering through the prairie.

"First, I would like to discover what exactly I could be doing outside my workplace. And this is S - specific. M - measurable ... I think I would like to specify in which time frames I could do it. And these time frames should be ambitious but realistic. Well ... On that we have to work. And I'd like to discover it during these our six sessions. And ... I still have to plan how to do it."

The coach reached for his notes.

"Listen, can we put it this way?" He began to read. "You want to find out what you could do

outside your work, which would fulfil the need of your heart and how much time could you devote to it. You also want to plan exactly how to accomplish these activities. And finally: you want to achieve it all during the next 6 sessions. How about it?"

"Exactly."

The coach smiled.

"In this situation, I'd like to set you homework, which will be the basis for us to work on during the next session. Can you write it down yourself? Describe exactly your childhood dreams about Winetou. We must discover what lies beneath your heart's need ... "

Be like Appache or a short guideline on the coaching pro-

What surprises Beata during the second meeting with the coach will be seen in the fifth chapter.

"AGAIN THE GOAL?"

The fifth chapter in which we start again from setting a goal and finding out why it's so important.

There were few people in the Theatre Cafe. Beata and the coach had taken the same table two weeks earlier. A wooden screen separating them from the rest of the room was enough to create an intimate atmosphere.

Waiting for the jasmine tea they had ordered, the coach started.

"We have about an hour. What would you like to achieve during today's session?"

Beata looked surprised.

"We already determined what I want to achieve on the previous meeting."

The coach began to explain.

"We set a goal that we want to achieve during our sessions. As you remember, the goal was complex. To recap; you want to find out what you could do outside work, which would fulfil your heart's need and how much time you could devote to it. You also want to plan exactly how you will accomplish these activities. And you want to achieve it during the next 6 sessions. This is your main goal. Now we have to start with something specific. That's why I asked you what you want to think about today."

"I think that for the beginning I want to determine how much time I can devote to the realisation of my dreams. I mean this need of my heart."

"Well." The coach pulled out his green notebook and pen.

Does Beata have time to implement her dreams? We'll find out in the sixth chapter.

"REALITY"

*The sixth chapter in which
we look at how Beata uses
her time and we will check
if her lifestyle allows her
to pursue her dreams.*

"**P**lease tell me how your day looks. How much time do you deal with particular matters?"

Beata sat more comfortably in the chair.

"I always get up around 6:00 in the morning. Then go to the toilet. Breakfast and then to work. On the way, I take my daughter to school. Usually I am in the office around 8.30. Then work to 18.00-19.00. Return home. Dinner with daughter, doing home-work lesson and ... sleep."

"Five days a week?"

"Yes. Five days a week. But sometimes I also work on Saturdays."

"On Saturdays? How often does that occur?"

"Usually one or two Saturdays a month."

"How many hours do you work on Saturdays?" The coach was interested in details.

"Shorter. Up to two o'clock, three o'clock in the afternoon. Sometimes I have a business dinner on a Saturday evening."

"Do you sometimes go on business trips?"

"Yes. I leave my home once or twice a month in Poland or abroad for two or three days. But usually business trips are during the week. Not on weekends."

The coach looked through his notes.

"Let's summarise. You work 5-6 days a week. Typically you do not have time in the evenings during the week for anything other than time with your daughter. You have 1-2 business trips in a month, but they are usually on weekdays, hence they do not interfere with your weekends." The coach looked over his notes. "Let's take the weekends then. How do you spend them?"

Beata thought about it.

"I usually deal with household matters. On Saturdays a cleaner comes to my apartment but I always help her. I do not sit still. Sometimes I visit friends.

My mother helps me with my daughter. Otherwise, I could not work. Sometimes I ask her to stay on Saturday evenings and then I have free time to myself. But then I feel guilty because I'm giving up this time with my daughter ..."

"We have arrived here at your beliefs and values. We'll come back to that in a moment. Tell me how else you spend time at weekends?"

"I go to church on Sunday mornings. Then dinner. We often eat with my parents. Then some time for fun with my daughter, book and bed."

"And what about trips to the lakes, the mountains, with a bit of madness?"

Beata smiled weakly.

"Looks like I grew out of it ..."

The coach did not comment.

"Please tell me, how much time you could devote to yourself at weekends?"

"From what I just told you, it seems that possibly quite a lot. In fact, half of Saturday and half of Sunday and maybe even the whole of Sunday I could have for myself if I do not bring work home, so basically I could use this time as I want. But..."

"But what?"

"I spend so little time with my daughter ... I do not want to reduce my time with her at weekends."

"As I said, what you're talking about is a matter of your values and beliefs. And this is extremely important. But before we get to them, let's answer the question we asked at the beginning of this session. How much time can you devote to pursue your own's

heart needs?"

"If you put it this way, the answer is one and a half days in the week."

In the next chapter will Beata accept that she really fully realises her life values.

"THE VALUES"

The seventh chapter shows how Beata understands her individual values and how it affects the level of satisfaction from her life.

"Y ou have a tool in front of you that is called 'a wheel of values'. Before we start to fill it, please look at a list of values and select the ones that matter most to you. Then think about any value important to you, which is not on this list. Well?"

"Of course." Beata raised her pen and started reading. From time to time she marked words on the page.

"Please, now choose the eight values that are the most important for you. What are these values?"

Beata began to enumerate.

"Respect, family, personal development, passion, joy, reliability, health, economic security.

Yes, these are the most important things for me."

"Now please, take this picture of a circle divided into 8 parts and enter the names of these

values of individual parts."

Beata performed the task.

"Now, please, paint part of each slice of the wheel corresponding to the given value to such an extent, in which you realise and perform this value in your life. Let us take as first personal development. Tell me what percent do you feel that you are satisfied in this regard?"

"Hmm. I think it's 90% good."

"In that case, paint over from the inside 90% of this slice. Well. Now do the same with the others."

After a long moment Beata managed to complete the task.

"Tell me please" the coach began. "What comes to mind looking at this picture?"

"Evidently I have deficiencies in the area of: passion, joy and family."

"How do you understand these values? Can you explain it to me?"

"Of course. Passion, that's my heart's need, this note

of madness in my life that I miss so much. I have marked 10%, and it is only because this 10% is filled by how I love my work. But it's not the same. I took the job into the personal development, and that one I pointed at 90%. Passion is a boat, it is wind in your hair, fresh breeze..."

"I see how your eyes shine when you talk about it..."

"That's because I miss it so much."

"Go on, please."

Beata brushed her hair back from her forehead.

"Well. The point 'Joy' I filled in with 50%. For me it means general joy, satisfaction with my life. On the one hand, I'm satisfied from what I've achieved, but on the other hand I'm still missing this something..."

After a moment, she continued.

"Family. Yes, the family is for me my daughter. Currently I'm just thinking about her. And a husband and marriage of course... if I meet some day someone special would be great. For now, however, the most important thing for me is my daughter. And I have the impression that I still do not fulfil myself as a mother. I spend too much time away from home, so I feel that I neglect it.

- I think we should talk about it now a little more. OK?

- OK...

Be like Appache or a short guideline on the coaching pro-

In the next chapter we will feel again the wind of adventure. Will Beata find the answer to the riddle, what is the need of her heart and how to meet it?

"DIRECTION, OR WHAT CAN I REALLY DO?"

The eighth chapter in which Beata begins to discover her dreams.

T he coach looked at his notes through a steaming cup of coffee. Outside the window it was a cold day. Maybe that's why there were more people in the cafe than usual.

"Today we are to think about what it is, this deep need in your heart? What is it that you miss so much?"

Beata looked into his eyes.

"It's good that we have previous sessions behind us.

It will certainly help me in meeting today's topic."

"Of course," agreed the coach. "Everything we have gone through so far was on purpose. Without knowing what is important to you or how much time you can sacrifice for the 'need of your heart', we would not have a chance to find and name it."

"Now, please list the things which could be considered as a 'nut of madness' if it happen to appear in your life" he added with a smile after a short break.

Beata closed her eyes and sat more comfortably in her chair.

"I'd like to sail. I could sail on lakes, seas." It seemed to him as in her voice he could hear the sound of waves.

"I would like to laugh and cry at the same time experiencing real happiness" she continued.

"I could also go skiing. Practically, every year I travel to Austria for skiing. But this is not a kind of little madness I miss – again she closed her eyes. - I could go to the lakes to sleep under a tent, with a boat moored in the harbour. Yes, that would be wonderful. Tent in the forest, picking mushrooms, stalking, playing with friends and daughter and then again water, sails."

"What else comes to your mind?"

"I could go on a cruise around the world."

"Interesting that you keep sails in your mind all the

time. Do you ever dream of a non-sailing dream?"

Beata thought for a long moment.

"I could sign up as a camp guardian nautical. Take my daughter there and inspire her with passion. Of course, it's also sailing," she added with a smile.

She was silent for a moment.

"Yes. I already know! Winnetou! Horses. Wigwam. I could start riding horses. Great idea."

"I have homework for you" the coach put something in his notebook.

"For next week visit, during your lunch time, bookstores and search for adventure books as well as travel books. Visit the nearest travel agencies and ask for interesting trips to exotic places. Try to do it every day and write down all the ideas that come to mind about things that you could do, or places that you could visit."

"Well. I like the idea."

How will Beata deal with her home task and will it lead her to finding the needs of her heart? We'll find out in the next chapter.

"THE CHOICE"

*The ninth chapter in which
we learn the method which
helped Beata to pass the
way from recognition of her
dreams to real knowledge
of the need of her heart.*

"**H**ow did you do your homework?"
Beata was 'all smiling'.

"I had great fun with it. The search itself gave me amazing joy. My mind wandered
around distant places. Dreams have reappeared. I
felt like a little girl again, except that this time together with the knowledge that these dreams are
within my reach. I have the resources to implement
them. The only question I have is: do I have enough
courage?"

"What dreams did you write down on your list?"

"I wrote a lot" her eyes were shining. "I made it choosing those that I think are real and of course ambitious" she smiled. "I remembered about SMART."

The coach nodded appreciatively.

"What did you choose?"

"I chose riding lessons with my daughter. Near to where we live is a stud. We could walk there every Saturday. I can buy a pass. Besides, I thought that I could go to the lakes once a month. I have found a small hut on the Internet by a bank of one lake. I also found a small sailboat I could buy. Just perfect for us, for me and my daughter. One more person also could fit in" she smiled.

"Did you pick anything else?"

Beata took her notebook from her purse, opened it and started to read.

"Meeting a group of friends and going on a monthly, holiday cruise on the Mediterranean. Purchase of a forester's lodge and weekly trips to create an 'Indian atmosphere'. I would invite friends there and together we could decorate our Wigwam, having great fun doing it. I could also buy a horse and keep it at the forester's lodge. I'd just have to find someone who would look after him during the week."

Beata was very pleased.

"How do you like my ideas?"

"The most important thing is that it should please you," the coach answered seriously. "My opinions can suggest you something and it would not be desirable. You would be the one living later with the consequences of this choice" he smiled. "Which of these ideas do you want to implement?"

"All!" - Beata laughed loudly. – "Of course I am kidding. But seriously, I could do some of them."

"Which, in that case, did you choose?"

"This is the most difficult question. I do not know which one to choose. I need your help."

The coach looked up.

"Let us apply then, the next of the coaching tools. Please write down on the sheet, one thing under the other, what you could do."

Beata concentrated on work in her notebook for a moment.

"Now write down the criteria according to which you can assess the accuracy of your choice. For example, the option of spending time with your daughter, the nut of madness, etc. You choose the criteria."

"Well. I have already chosen."

"Write these criteria one below the other. Now we will put weights on them. What is more important to you; time spent with your daughter or this 'nut of madness', how have you named it?"

"Time spent with my daughter."

"In that case write '1' for 'time spent with daughter' and '0' for 'nut of madness'."

"Now tell me what is more important to you; time spent with your daughter or time spent with friends?"

"Time spent with my daughter."

The coach nodded.

"In that case, put again '1' for 'time spent with daughter' and '0' for 'time with friends'. Now answer what is more important to you; a nut of madness or time with your friends?"

"Hmm. It's harder. I think a nut of madness."

" So write '1' for 'nut of madness' and '0' for 'time with friends'."

"Done."

The coach looked at Beata's notebook.

"What did you get? Please, summarise all the points. So you have '2' for 'time spent with daughter', '1' for 'nut of madness' and '0' for 'time with friends'. Therefore, we have two criteria that have obtained weight greater than 0. Save them, please, in the form of columns on the list of your possibilities. Done?"

"Yes."

"Now we will do a similar exercise with your chosen ideas. But this time we will refer them to your criteria."

"OK."

"Which will allow you to feel more madness: horse riding lessons, or buying a cottage at the lakes?"

"Buying a cottage at the lakes. Definitely!"

"Save '1' for 'hut' and '0' for 'horse lessons'. Done?"

"Yes."

"Later, we will multiply these ones by one in the column 'Nut of madness' and by 2 in the 'time with daughter'. Do you understand the principle now?"

"Of course. Let's continue ..."

"What did you get?" The coach asked after several minutes.

"It took a while because we included two additional criteria, but it was worth the effort. The results of the job surprised me a bit."

"Which idea has won?" The coach demanded.

"'The 'hut at the lakes' runs with 20 points. In second place is a monthly cruise on the Mediterranean Sea, which scored 17 points. Other possibilities are further behind.

"How do you feel with it?"

"Good," Beata said calmly. "Actually, now I see that I could really do these two things in my life. For others there is no space but I probably no longer need to implement them. If I buy a hut at the lakes, a sailboat and every year organize a fantastic cruise with my close friends, it would definitely increase the feeling that this hidden need of my heart is now fulfilled. Because these two are really the needs my heart" She smiled broadly, realising that she has just found what she was looking for.

Will realisation of these dreams really bring satisfaction to the life of Beata? We'll check it in the next chapter in which we run out somewhat in the future.

"VISION."

The tenth chapter in which Beata tries to see what is not there yet to gain the certainty that this is what she wants.

"**I**f you have already chosen what you want to do, then please let us do one more exercise."

Beata looked up from her notebook.

"What do you mean?"

"Please, sit down comfortably" the coach waited a moment so she could take a more comfortable position in the chair. "Close your eyes and start listening to your breathing. Focus on it. Inhale ... Exhale ... Inhale ... Exhale ... Calm down."

"Now imagine that two years already passed. You do have your hut at the lakes. You just came back from a cruise on the Mediterranean where you have been with your friends. You are now on your sailing boat. The water is calm, the sun is shining. Have you moved already yourself into the future?

"Yes," Beata answered somewhat absently.

"Tell me then please, what do you see?"

"I see myself, I see my daughter who is smiling to me and she is sitting at the steering wheel. I am also happy and fulfilled. I can hear birds singing and the sound of waves."

"How do you feel with it?"

"Excellent."

"Was it worth trying to accomplish all this? Looking for the right place, spending money on a hut and a boat? Taking the time to organise your trip in the Mediterranean?"

"Oh yes. It was definitely worth it."

"How much do you assess your fulfilment in the piece called 'passion'?"

"At 100%!"

"Thank you. You can come back to today. Welcome back to our theatre cafe. It is Wednesday, no vacation." The coach added with a laugh.

"OKAY. I'm already back. What a pleasant exercise."

Will it still be so nice when Beata confronts the

Be like Appache or a short guideline on the coaching pro-

compatibility of her new goals with important ideas for her values? About that in the eleventh chapter.

"ECOLOGY, OR HOW I WILL LIVE WITH IT."

Eleventh chapter, which shows whether the implementation of Beata's goals will not disturb her 'ecosystem', or how it will affect her important values.

"**D**o you remember how we worked on your values?"

Beata nodded. She drank coffee from a white porcelain cup.

"Of course. I even remember which one I chose."

"That's great." The coach opened his green note-book.

"Let's check now if your choice is an ecological one."

"Ecological? What does it mean?"

"We'll check if the goals you set up will not nega-tively affect some other, important for you, value."

Beata looked up.

"It makes sense. So what if I'm achieving my own dreams, if my family suffers. That's it?"

"Exactly," agreed the coach. "So let's get back to the values you have chosen. For this we'll use again a circle divided like an orange into 8 parts. Fill each of these parts again with the name of the specified value.

Beata prepared the diagram very accurately.

"I already have."

"Insert now please, plus and minus signs for each of the values you chose, depending on what impact your new plans will have on each of them."

A delicate wrinkle appeared on Beata's forehead.

After a moment she looked up.

"I have already done this exercise."

"I am listening."

"Six values got plus and two got zeros."

"What do the zeros mean?"

"Neutral influence. I set zero for personal development and economic security. I believe that realisation of my dreams will not affect these elements in any way."

"Are you sure about that? Think carefully. In general, everything we do, all our decisions have lesser or greater impact on almost all the realm of our life, whether we realise it or not."

"I do not know ..." Beata apparently had doubts.

"Let's take a look at this from a different perspective. If you go on a vacation for a month, for this wonderful cruise on the Mediterranean, will it affect your work in any way? If yes, please tell me in which?

"Hmm" Beata thought loudly. – If I leave for a whole month, then someone will have to replace me. But I have such a person and I am able to prepare everything so that she can effectively perform work entrusted to her. You know, summer time is dead season here. Usually nothing is really happening. And if anything does happen, I have a phone. I can arrange that every day I would call from the port to make sure everything is fine. It's a good idea."

"You are still convinced that it will not have any impact on the situation at your workplace and your professional development?"

"Certainly not negative" she replied with certainty

in her voice. "It can even have a positive impact as I would develop one of my employees while I am resting and happy, which should also have a positive effect on my later efficiency. By the way, I wrote 'Personal development'. It's much more than just 'professional'" - in Beata's voice sounded a slight reprimand.

"Of course you are right. I'm sorry" the coach smiled.

"I think I can easily write a plus for it."

"So we have only one more value in this situation with zero influence?"

"Yes. Maybe I should think about it again ." Beata was not so sure of it now. "I have enough days of leave, saved from the previous year. I do not have to take unpaid leave. In our company they look at me with understanding. After all, my boss goes on trips around the United States every year. Usually, these are three whole weeks."

Beata laughed.

"I think it can even have a positive impact on our relationship and my position. The boss will understand my need of a little 'craziness' in my life, because he owns it himself. We will have more in common. I will be more satisfied and effective at work upon my return from such vacation. All this can contribute to my further promotion. Again plus."

The coach also laughed.

"So we have eight pluses."

"Yes."

"What we have achieved now is the confidence that our dreams and choices are consistent with our values. And this is one of the most important things in taking any decisions.

What - in addition to compliance with the values - will facilitate Beata to accomplish the goal, and what can make it difficult? About this in the next chapter.

"RESOURCES AND OBSTACLES."

Twelfth chapter in which Beata identifies the resources that may help in implementation of the goal and possible obstacles along the way.

T he waiter went away with the order. They ordered, as usual, two cups of coffee with milk.

"Today we will deal with what will help you in your implementation of the goal and what might stand in your way."

"Sounds good" Beata nodded. "You mean; who can help me organise the cruise and buy a house by the lake?

"That too," the coach nodded. "We will consider, which of your current resources will enable you to implement this dream and what is it that you still need."

"Fine."

"First question: Do you have anything that will enable you to purchase a house at the lakes, a sailing boat and organisation of a cruise on the Mediterranean?"

"Let's think" She gently bit her lips thoughtfully. "I have enough financial resources."

"I will put it in my notes. OK?" the coach interrupted.

"Yes of course. What's next?" She wondered looking at the ceiling. "I've found a hut on the internet and a boat that I would like to buy. Of course I will check it out and be look a little bit more. I have a friend in the real estate business, who can help me to find a beautiful place which would suit me."

"I have it. What else do you have?"

"I also have a friend in a travel agency who can help me organise a cruise. Her name is Katie."

"Something else?"

"I have my daughter's support. She liked my ideas very much. And that means a lot to me. That's probably so much for resources."

The coach drew a line in the notebook.

"Now, please tell me what may disturb you in the implementation of this vision?"

"Hmm. Let me think about it" Beata for a moment thought in silence.

"I think that I will need to receive a whole month vacation. With this there may be a problem. It will set a precedent in the company."

"How will you deal with it?"

"I'll go to my boss and try to convince him."

"What arguments will you use?"

"I'll say I need a trip to recharge my batteries and that I will be more efficient upon my return. First, I'll ask him about his journeys ..." She smiled "I will also say that in the case of a cruise, four weeks is an ideal period of time for such an activity."

"Why is four weeks the perfect period?"

"The renting of a boat is an issue. The journey itself there and back would take several days. I need at least two days at the beginning and at the end to organise myself and get there. It all means that we will spend only three weeks on the yacht."

"I understand. And what happens if the boss does not agree? What will you do then?"

"In the worst case, he will agree to three weeks. Then I will fly by plane and I will have only four hours for preparation for our travel. But I'll manage it." She laughed loudly.

"What else can prevent you from achieving your goal?"

"Nothing else comes to my mind ..."

Will Beata's dreams come true so smoothly? We'll find out in the next section.

"HOW WILL I DO IT? WHEN WILL I DO IT?"

Thirteenth chapter, in which Beata starts to translate her intentions into concrete steps and action plan.

"So now, we can determine the steps, what you have to do to achieve your goals. Can I ask you to get up?"

The coach rose from his chair. Beata, a bit surprised, followed him.

"The cafe is empty, so we will not surprise anyone with what we're about to do. Please, stand here. Close your eyes and imagine that a year has passed.

You're just lying on the wooden floor of an yacht on the Mediterranean. In Poland a sailboat is waiting for you, moored at your beautiful cottage by the lake. Do you see it?"

"Yes, I can see it." Beata was smiling.

"Now take a step back and say what must have happened just before this wonderful moment?"

"Hmm. I had to organise a trip."

"What does it mean in particular?"

"I had to buy plane tickets to get to Croatia. I bought tickets for the cruise. I found it earlier so I got the best offer. And I organised a crew before."

"I understand. So now step back one more step. What had to happen beforehand?"

"Oh. So it means I have already organised a cruise" Beata was standing with her eyes still closed. "I got along with the boss earlier that I will get a thirty-day holiday in July. I also had to prepare a person who will replace me at that time."

"Please go back a step. What should happen right now?"

"I should close the matter with buying a house at the lake and a boat. Although I can do it simultaneously with a conversation with my boss and finding a deputy."

"I understand that at this point you made a purchase of a hut and a boat?"

"Yes," she agreed. "I'm just closing the transaction."

"Take a step back then. What happened before?"

"I searched the internet, talked to Danusia from the real estate agency. I made a choice regarding the investment."

"Did something have to happen before?"

"No. Earlier it is today." She laughed.

The coach shifted slightly to the side.

"You can open your eyes now. Go again all the way from the beginning of the cruise, to sort out all the steps."

"OK."

Beata walked energetically for the next few minutes on the floor of a cafe. The waiter watching her from behind the curtain decided not to leave the back room. Anyway, in the room – except the coach and Beata - there was not a soul.

"Note all the steps in the notebook now" the coach's voice interrupted a long silence.

"OKAY." Beata sat down and began writing in her notebook.

"Tell me when will you complete the next steps?"

"Do you want me to set dates now?" she asked, a little surprised by the imposed pace.

"Yes. What is your first step?"

"Contact the real estate office."

"When will you contact Danusia?" the coach asked.

"Hmm. Even tomorrow."

"Save it, please ..."

Will the plan that was made during this meeting be implemented? We'll find out it by reading the next, fourteenth chapter.

"CELEBRATION OF SUCCESS"

Fourteenth chapter in which we find out what Beata managed to achieve after a month from the time of establishing an action plan.

"**A** month has passed since our last meeting" the coach began. "Did you do anything from what we had planned?"

"Oh, yes" Beata was smiling broadly. "On Friday I finalised the purchase of a home at the lakeside.

"Great! Do you have photos?"

"Of course!"

For the next few minutes the coach and Beata were

busy looking at photos.

"What else did you manage to accomplish?"

"I received my boss's permission for 30 days leave. It was not easy."

"Congratulations. How did you convince him?"

"I used the arguments that we formulated during our previous meetings. He agreed that as a woman with a child I need a bit more time than he needs to prepare such a trip. It took me two meetings. But he finally agreed."

"Have you already chosen a cruise?"

"No, not yet, but I'm working on it."

"What do you mean?"

"I contacted a colleague, who showed me a few suggestions. I have not decided yet ..."

At that moment, the waiter came.

"I think we both deserve a coffee and a big cookie today. What do you think about it?"

"Of course," Beata answered.

"Celebrating successes, even minor ones, and in this case you were very successful, is an extremely important element of coaching. And not only for coaching."

"Oh, yes" she nodded, smiling all the time. "It builds you up and gives you energy for further action."

Be like Appache or a short guideline on the coaching pro-

"Double cup?"

Successes can only be celebrated if you are on your way to achieving your goal. In the next chapter we will find out what to do when there is a lack of this goal.

"WHEN THERE IS NO GOAL."

The fifteenth chapter in which we find out how to help a person who does not know where they are going.

"I have a friend" Beata started the conversation, "who evidently needs coaching."

"She is invited" the coach smiled.

"Yes, I know." She paused for a moment. "The problem is that she does not know what she really wants. And I remember, as you said at the beginning of our work, that to make sure that the coaching process makes sense, the person being coached should know the question they are trying to find the answer to. It makes sense, but ..."

"But what?"

'But I'm convinced that my friend needs coaching. However, when I ask her a question: what does she mean, what does she need, she could not give me any answer."

"What convinces you that your friend needs coaching?"

"She's been sad for some time. She says that nothing gives her joy anymore, that she is missing something..."

"There are two possibilities," the coach said seriously. "Or your friend just started suffering from depression and a coach will not help her. In that case she should go to a psychologist or a doctor. Or indeed she needs coaching, but she just cannot specify what it is that she really needs. In this situation a coach could help her."

"This is not depression. I'm sure of it. I've seen people depressed. She just needs coaching. Can you help her? Maybe you know some way to find out what it is that she needs but cannot specify it?"

"First of all she needs to go to a doctor to make sure that she has no depression. Regarding the latter question, I won't give you a simple answer; as it should be in a coaching" he replied after a moment silence. "Our sessions, putting it very simply, proceeded according to the scheme defined by the acronym GROW. Does it remind you anything at all?"

"No. Explain please."

"The scheme consists of four stages in which the answer to the main coaching question is found and you achieve the purpose of our meetings. G means goal. Goal. At this stage it is good to determine what we want to achieve at the end of coaching. Next R or reality. Reality."

"To understand where are we today?"

"Yes. Where we are today. How your reality looks associated with a specific topic on which we are working."

Beata listened intently.

"Then we have O or options. Possibilities. At this stage, we should determine what options we have on the way of accomplishing our goal."

"I recognise all these stages. You passed through them with me. Correct?"

"Of course. These and other things. We are talking here about the very basic scheme. We are left now with W."

"Ways I guess? We need to decide at this point, what we have to do now?"

"You guessed right. At this stage, we discuss what actions you have to take to achieve the goal. Only the letter "W" in this acronym means What Next, meaning what you should do next. But the meaning is the same."

"I understand."

The coach smiled. Then he pulled his green note-book and in large letters wrote: "GROW".

"Look at these letters. Tell me what we can do in a situation where we cannot start with G or the goal, because the person who is a subject to coaching is not able to define it?"

Beata thought for a moment. She bent over the page, raised her pen and wrote RGOW.

"We can start with a conversation. From what it looks like the reality in which a given person is now. How happy she is, how many changes she needs."

"Well done" the coach was pleased. "Exactly. In that situation we start from R, from reality, and then we pass to G; goal, purpose. The moment we talk about what the current situation looks like, people usu-ally start to see their dreams and ideas for how they would like to see their reality tomorrow. And those dreams are ours goals of coaching sessions."

"So you have another client ..."

As you can see, there is no hopeless situation and even without knowing the purpose at the outset, you can take advantage from coaching. The next chapter will briefly remind us what exactly the coaching process consists of.

"LET'S SUMMARISE."

*The sixteenth chapter in which
Beata enquires, what really
happened from the moment
of the first meeting with
the coach. Let's once again
go through this path.*

"**D**ear Coach ..." Beata clearly changed her tone. They were sitting in the same cafe again, celebrating another of her success.

"Oh, oh. What an introduction! I start to hear you carefully. "The coach did not hide his curiosity.

"You recently told me about the GROW scheme, saying that we have gone through these elements and a few others as well. It intrigued me. Could you tell me, what did we actually do during our sessions?"

"Of course. Let us recall everything from beginning. OKAY?"

"Sure. I remember we started with the contract."

"Yes. What else?"

"And from accepting you as a coach, in the coaching contract we talked about you being responsible for the process and me for the result of coaching."

"Exactly. Why should you answer for the result of the session?"

"Because we assumed that I have everything that is important and needed to achieve the goal we set ourselves."

"Everything is perfectly correct" the coach smiled. "What was next?"

"We've talked about the different types of coaching and reasons why people ask for coaching."

"It was like that. Do you remember my answers?"

"I think so. Operational coaching is the one at work. True?"

"Yes. The coach observes the client in his natural environment. It serves the development of individual competences and skills."

"This is it. Then holistic coaching. Life and business."

"In companies, if it concerns managerial staff, we call it executive coaching. You remember the reason people usually ask to coaching?"

Beata was gathering her thoughts for a moment.

"To find the answer to questions to which they cannot answer by themselves?"

"Exactly. This is the case, for example, in a situation of change, promotion, life events. And sometimes is that just in this moment we need changes."

"Like me," Beata said with a smile.

"That's right. Do you remember what we did later?"

Beata fell into a pensive mood.

"After determining the purpose of the session, we defined the specific goal for each session. We discussed reality, or how things are today. Then we were wondering what we would like this reality to look like in the future."

"We took care of our values on the way," the coach interjected.

"It was very valuable. It allowed me to sort out what's most important in my life. And then, once we made our choices, we could verify how my decisions would affect these values."

"In this way, we determined the consistency of your goals with your values."

"We also checked the ecology of the goal. Do I remember the name of it well?"

"Very good," the coach confirmed. "We examined how much the implementation of your intentions can have a negative impact to other areas of your life."

"Fortunately, it turned out that the implementation of my dreams can only affect my life positively." A big smile did not leave Beata's face.

"What happened next?"

"We discussed my resources or what will help me accomplish my plans" she replied, sipping coffee. "Then we took care of the obstacles that I can meet on my way. Well, we finally agreed the steps I need to take to reach my goal. We also planned the exact dates I intend to put them into practice?"

"And we celebrated success."

They both laughed.

On the way to achieving the goal, Beata met important values. Can she also get to know better herself during coaching?

About this in the next chapter.

"WHO AM I? METAPHOR AND PERSONALITY PROFILE"

The seventeenth chapter in which we find out what has in common with Beata's personality Pocahontas and the sound of a saxophone.

"**I**s there any tool that allows me better understand myself?"

"In principle, the coaching process itself opens our eyes to a lot of information about ourselves," the coach said after consideration. "After all, we touch our values, beliefs. However, if I had to mention any tools helpful in this process, I would mention two, in my opinion, the most effective. Metaphors and personality profiles."

Beata raised her eyebrows.

"Metaphors? I understand the personality profiles, after all, they serve this purpose. But metaphors?"

The coach straightened in his chair.

"Metaphors activate our subconscious" he began to explain gesticulating. "They let us reach these layers of knowledge about ourselves, which we often do not even expect. Let's make an example. Can you identify with any fairy tale character?"

"From a fairy tale? Which fairy tale?"

"No matter. What comes to mind first?"

Beata thought about it for a moment.

"I think Pocahontas."

"Why Pocahontas?"

"Because, like her, I am full of life and energy myself. I can manage my life well and I am protective. If someone gets in the circle of my influence, I really can fight for him and protect him."

"Now focus. What kind of sound do you associate with?"

"Sound? It's crazy ... But let's try" Beata focused. "Maybe with the sound of a saxophone?" "Why a saxophone?"

"I do not know. It was just the first thing that came to mind."

"Try a bit harder" encouraged the coach. "Why the sound of saxophone?"

"Okay. Because is soft, nice to listen to and it's so in order and in fullness. It gives me peace. It works" she laughed.

"You see" the coach was very serious. "Metaphors activate the right cerebral hemisphere, responsible for creativity and intuition. Performing such break-neck exercise, like with the sound of a saxophone, we force our mind to do illogical activities, through which we release the layers of the subconscious. Are you identifying with the terms you used?"

"Yes. And what about personality tests?" Beata was curious.

"There are many professional personality profiles available on the market. I'm not talking about these internet games with free tests. These should be treated rather as entertainment, and you can find many on the internet or in newspapers. I'm talking about professional tests."

"Is it expensive?"

"Everything is relative. If I use it during coach-ing, then the client does not pay extra for a pro-file. Everything is included in the price of coaching. Thank you for the time we had together. It was very

Be like Appache or a short guideline on the coaching pro-

inspiring also for me.

"Thank you."

The end.
Artur Tołłoczko

www.ingramcontent.com/pod-product-compliance
Lightning Source LLC
Chambersburg PA
CBHW030952240526
45463CB00016B/2518